'Compassionate, hopef for all Christians and a great help as we navigate the vital issues around sexuality.'
Gavin Calver, CEO, Evangelical Alliance

'Whether you are confused or frustrated, scared or scarred, Ed Shaw's latest book will help you to find a renewed sense of joy and purpose for your God-given sexuality. Armed with a better understanding of God's purpose for our sexuality, Ed shows how we will be better equipped to navigate the trials and temptations of our sex-obsessed world. It's a book I will be recommending to people in all kinds of different situations.'
Ros Clarke, Associate Director, Church Society

'In this compelling short read, Ed Shaw poses the question, "What is the purpose of our sexuality?" With courageous honesty, he mines deep into Scripture and brings some incredible gems to light. He unearths how our sexuality is the most graphic imagery for the passion and potency of God's love. Sheer dynamite!'
The Rt Revd Dr Jill Duff, Anglican Bishop of Lancaster

'How can such a short book pack such a punch? With humanity and great humility, Ed Shaw shows us why our sexuality is such a good thing. That God in his kindness has given us a way to feel the passion of his love for us and yearn for more of him. And that this is for all of us, in all our mess, whether or not we're married.'
Mark Ellis, Director of Christian Unions Ireland

'This wise, sensitive book has a great deal to offer all of us as we attend to the desires, questions and struggles arising

from our nature as sexual beings. Its contemporary frame of reference, combined with careful reading of relevant biblical texts, makes it all the more valuable.'
Julian Hardyman, Senior Pastor, Eden Baptist Church, Cambridge, and author of *Jesus, Lover of my Soul*

'We live in times when things we know and values we hold are changing and in flux. From our humanity to our identity, everything seems up for redefinition. Perhaps it's at the point of our sexuality that this is most vivid and complex. With brilliant clarity, grace-filled empathy and biblical truth, Ed Shaw helps us to understand the plan and purpose of our sexuality and wisely draws us back to the place of healing and redemption we all truly need.'
Tope Koleoso, Lead Pastor, Jubilee Church, London

'I am so thankful that I am a sexual being! Ed's book is a much needed hurricane of fresh air on the purpose of sexuality. As a single heterosexual woman, I am once more staggered by God's kindness in crafting me with sexual desire so that I may more tangibly appreciate his love for me. Ed's short book is beautifully biblical, richly pastoral and deeply evocative. A glorious vision of human flourishing is to be found within these pages. I am *more* for having read this.'
Kristi Mair, Research Fellow in Philosophy, Ethics and Apologetics at Oak Hill Theological College, author and speaker

'"Sex is life" advertising slogans hit us constantly. But what kind of sex really is "life"? A colossal crisis in relationships and a profound loneliness seem to be the outcomes of this pansexual society. The so-called "sexual revolution" has not

brought the flourishing life it promised, but rather the opposite. In this concise and clear book, Ed Shaw shows how the biblical vision for sexuality is indeed a source of life and fulfilment. The book provides a lucid and solid framework on sexuality for everyone, but especially for those who are frustrated, confused and tired of the "paradise" promised by secular views.'
Dr Pablo Martinez, psychiatrist, author and Bible teacher

'For a contentedly single heterosexual woman, I seem to be reading a lot of books about sex and sexuality these days. It is a vital topic, and something I need to have a clear, biblical understanding of as someone involved in pastoral work – and indeed as someone involved in human life! *Purposeful Sexuality* is a brief but vital addition to the genre. In this excellent little book, Ed reveals a deep understanding both of the questions surrounding sexuality and of the Bible's glorious, hopeful, life-giving answers. How is God's gift of sexuality good news for all of us, whatever our circumstances? Read this book to find out.
Jennie Pollock, Associate Head of Public Policy, Christian Medical Fellowship, and author of *If Only*

'A short, clear and often profound book on one of our generation's most pressing subjects. Ed Shaw has served us superbly with *Purposeful Sexuality*.'
Andrew Wilson, Teaching Pastor, King's Church London, and author of *If God, Then What?*

PURPOSEFUL SEXUALITY

A short Christian introduction

Ed Shaw

INTER-VARSITY PRESS
36 Causton Street, London SW1P 4ST, England
Email: ivp@ivpbooks.com
Website: www.ivpbooks.com

The author and publisher have made every effort to ensure that the external
website addresses included in this book are correct and up to date at the time
of going to press. The author and publisher are not responsible for the content,
quality or continuing accessibility of the sites.

Scripture quotations are taken from The Holy Bible, New International Version
(Anglicized edition). Copyright © 1979, 1984, 2011 by Biblica. Used by permission
of Hodder & Stoughton Ltd, an Hachette UK company. All rights reserved.'NIV'
is a registered trademark of Biblica. UK trademark number 1448790.

First published in 2021

British Library Cataloguing-in-Publication Data
A catalogue record for this book is available from the British Library.

ISBN: 978-1-78974-283-1
eBook ISBN: 978-1-78974-311-1

10 9 8 7 6 5 4 3 2 1

Set in Minion Pro 11.5/14.75 pt
Typeset in Great Britain by CRB Associates, Potterhanworth, Lincolnshire

*Inter-Varsity Press publishes Christian books that are true to the Bible and
that communicate the gospel, develop discipleship and strengthen the church
for its mission in the world.*

*IVP originated within the Inter-Varsity Fellowship, now the Universities and Colleges
Christian Fellowship, a student movement connecting Christian Unions in universities
and colleges throughout Great Britain, and a member movement of the International
Fellowship of Evangelical Students. Website: www.uccf.org.uk. That historic
association is maintained, and all senior IVP staff and committee members
subscribe to the UCCF Basis of Faith.*

To all those who have talked about sexuality with me.
Thank you.

Contents

Introduction:
What are we talking about?

One of my favourite writers, William Maxwell, begins a short story entitled 'What Every Boy Should Know' with these words: 'Shortly before his twelfth birthday, Edward Gellert's eyes were opened and he knew he was naked.'[1] He's describing that moment in life when someone discovers for the very first time that they possess an 'ability to experience or express sexual feelings',[2] that they have, according to that dictionary definition, a sexuality. You may or may not remember when that happened for you.[3]

Our human capacity for sexual feelings is the broad definition of sexuality that we will be using throughout this book as we seek to form a Christian understanding and appreciation of them. But, as we begin this journey, it is worth recognizing that talk of something called sexuality is relatively new – the *Oxford English Dictionary* dates its first use in the English language to 1879.[4] So we will be reading the language of sexual experience and feelings through-out the Bible in the light of a recently invented catch-all term rather than turning to a three-point sermon that Jesus gave on the subject of human sexuality.

Most of the time I will speak of sexuality in the singular because this short introduction is written to be as relevant as possible to as many as possible. I want to address sexuality as an almost universal human experience that unites us, rather than as something that divides us into multiple different groups. That said, there are going to be many times (especially in the first chapter) when we need to recognize very different experiences and expressions of sexuality, and then I will speak about sexualities in the plural.

It will help you to know that I write as a Christian man who is same-sex attracted, or gay. But this is not primarily a book about my sexuality in a personal sense (I've written that already[5]). It is instead a short introduction to sexuality in as universal a sense as is humanly possible. Because this is such a brief attempt, we will inevitably skate over much, but I'm hoping that my introductory big-picture thinking will provoke deeper (and better) thinking and discussion in other places. At the end of the book there are questions for reflection that might help kick-start this – note that these should be used at the end of *each* chapter.

To state the obvious: thinking about sexuality may well trigger painful memories for some of us. Do take your time – and read on in good company if that would help. My prayer is that this short book will bring you some comfort, as well as challenge you, as we all increasingly seek to embrace our Creator God's good gift of purposeful sexuality.

1

Why is talking about sexuality so difficult?

Have you ever been part of a conversation where you thought you were all talking about the same experience, person or thing, and then suddenly realized you weren't at all? A few minutes in, someone provided more details, and you found that what you thought you had in common you didn't after all: he or she had actually lived in a very different part of town, they hadn't met your cousin at that party, and they didn't love the same track on that album. The conversation descended into mutual confusion, then some mild embarrassment, and you each chose to make a quick exit soon after. It happens to me all the time – please reassure me that I am not alone!

We all have unique sexualities

Our rare conversations around sexuality, our capacity for sexual feelings, can be a bit like that. Because people often use the same words, we can too quickly presume that we are talking about the same experiences, and then suddenly realize how different things have been for others. This happened to me quite a lot when I first came out as gay (in a slightly alternative Christian way), and started talking to other same-sex-attracted friends about what I presumed were similar life experiences. It turned out that there was much we shared, but then one of us would say something and be met with looks of utter incomprehension from the others, the confusion and embarrassment made worse by our being a group of repressed Englishmen already far outside our comfort zones.

Since then I've started speaking much more honestly and publicly about sexuality, and I've been made to realize again and again that we all have unique experiences, that no-one's experience of sexuality is ever the same as anyone else's. This makes good communication on the subject a real challenge for all of us. We think we are speaking the same language, desiring the same sorts of things, but we aren't, and this leads to confusion (and embarrassment) again and again, and often to a sudden wish to start talking about the weather instead.

At one level, this shouldn't have been so much of a surprise to me – or anyone else. Just think of this relatively common scenario: someone is trying to match up a friend with a colleague whom they think is incredibly good looking. They locate a photo on Facebook, but the friend immediately rejects the handsome colleague: 'He's not my type.' One woman thought a colleague was drop-dead gorgeous, while another didn't give him a second look. We all fancy different people, and even have phrases for quickly explaining that to others: 'not my type'. In that sort of context we are not unused to communicating the idea that we feel different things, are attracted to different people and have very different sexualities.

It's this range of experiences that best explains the constant proliferation of identity markers in our culture today: why we have moved so quickly from inventing the very concept of sexuality to the simplicity of the binary heterosexual or homosexual labels, to distinguishing sub-groups of lesbian or gay (LG), to adding bisexual (LGB), to recognizing transgender (LGBT), to including queer (LGBTQ), not forgetting intersex (LGBTQI), and to avoiding the risk of leaving anyone else out (LGBTQI+).[1] It turns out that many people are looking for exactly the right word or letter to sum up their sexual desires (and other related feelings), and are finding that it's sometimes easier to make up a new one or just to opt for a fluidity that gives them the freedom to move around them all.[2] We are all uniquely wired sexually, and all of us will have a unique range of sexual experiences throughout our lives that will shape us in different ways.

All of this makes it a challenge whenever we try to sit down and talk about sexuality with anyone. We can think we're talking about the same thing but we're not. We think that other people have shared all our experiences but they haven't. As a result, we need to be clearer in our communication and to take more care to listen than in almost any other context today. I've had hundreds (perhaps thousands) of conversations around sexuality in the last few years and, having got things wrong so often, I've been reminded of this again and again. So please expect this short book to be more complicated and challenging than its size might lead you to expect. Especially because there's more to it than that: we don't just all have unique sexualities.

We all have uniquely damaged sexualities

There will be people reading these words whose sexuality has been uniquely and tragically damaged by sexual abuse when they were children, by unlooked-for exposure to online pornography as teenagers or by a first painful experience of sexual intercourse as an adult. We carry around emotional scars, perhaps even huge gaping wounds, from what was done to us in the past. And this, of course, makes any conversation about sexuality even harder. It injects so much pain into the discussion, and perhaps reignites feelings of shame that we hoped had died away. Too many people I have spoken to struggle to feel that any of their sexual feelings are good, or to confidently distinguish what sexual behaviour is right or wrong, because of what was cruelly done to them by others.

One of the most famous hashtags of recent years has been #MeToo, which has been used by countless women since 2017 to share the damage inflicted on them and their sexuality (usually by more powerful men). In far too many contexts, the power dynamic between a man with the ability to hire or fire and a woman he wants to have sex with has left that woman (and her career) irreparably damaged. It is right that many of these men (the film producer Harvey Weinstein being a prominent example) have now had their own careers and reputations ruined in return. The sexual revolution that was supposed to free women from being treated as sexual objects in the home has too often given men the cultural freedom to treat women like sexual objects everywhere else as well.

All of this means that some of us will always struggle to talk about sexuality because our sexuality has been so badly damaged. I guess all of us will sadly be able to point to ways in which perhaps just a small comment or careless action has injured our sexuality. I know I'm not alone, for example, in having a body image that has been harmed by our culture's narrow and unrealistic definition of what makes someone sexually desirable. We all have unique sexualities *and* we all have uniquely damaged sexualities. And then, to complicate things even further . . .

We all have uniquely damaging sexualities

All of us will have used or expressed our sexualities in ways that have damaged others, sometimes repeating the very damage that was inflicted on us. For some of us, it may be in obviously horrific ways that have left someone else permanently scarred as a result of our abusive behaviour, or it might be the tragedy of an abortion. As a result, we get this point all too easily, and for years we have been bitterly regretting the damage our sexuality has caused.

Perhaps most of us have been quietly damaging others in smaller ways that have gone unnoticed by others, and perhaps unrepented of by us. We have sex, or withhold it, as part of some selfish power play within our marriage. We regularly access pornography online, fuelling an industry that has left many of its trafficked 'actors' addicted to sex and drugs. We have had unrealistic expectations of love and romance, determined more by Hollywood romcoms than by realistic expectations. We have noticed that someone is attracted to us, but have not told them of our lack of interest in them because we enjoy the ego boost of having their eyes follow us around the room.

Then there is the reality that these behaviours damage us too – we have been sexually self-harming for years. Some of us have no-one else to blame for the sexual dysfunction brought about by our pornography addiction and compulsive masturbation. I know that many of my own sexual wounds have been self-inflicted, through what I've chosen to do with my body or dwell on in my mind.

When it comes to sexuality, almost every adult on this planet is both a victim *and* a victimizer to a greater or lesser extent. While, on the whole, most men have a worse track record than most women, it is not only men who damage women sexually, and it is not only in heterosexual relationships that damage is done. Different generations have had different patterns of damaging sexual behaviour: we're too good at overreacting to the damage caused by the previous generation in newly damaging ways. One generation self-harmed through sexual repression, the next through sexual liberation – and back the pendulum swings. At a more personal level, we can be so self-righteously blind to our hypocrisy, publicly criticizing the sexual objectification of people in a film in one moment, then mentally undressing the person who walks past us in the next. The result is that . . .

We all need help

Other people have made a mess of us, and we have contributed to making a mess of others – and ourselves. And, because everyone is implicated in this mess, it can feel as if we have nowhere to turn for the help we all so obviously need. The theologian Ephraim Radner has summarized our shared human predicament well: 'we do not really have any clear standpoint of experiential purity from which to figure the topic of sexuality out'.[3] Left to ourselves, we are in trouble. In the world around us, people who were until recently held up as models of sexual liberation to learn from have now been exposed as sexual predators to avoid. The same has been true of some who have preached sexual morality within our churches: they were privately doing themselves what they publicly condemned in others. In such a context, which of us is foolhardy enough to offer ourselves as a wise and honest authority on the subject? As another theologian, Jessica Martin, honestly puts it, 'I am a player, not an observer, in a field of extraordinary complexity.'[4] And I'm certainly not saying in this book, 'I've got it all right – follow me!' Quite the opposite! I have made, and continue to make, a right mess of myself (and others) with my own uniquely damaged and damaging sexuality.

The Bible's story, of course, helps us make sense of all this in the episode it relates in Genesis chapters 1 – 3. It tells of humanity being made good (which accounts for our longing for goodness in all its forms), but soon after choosing to reject goodness for evil (which explains how evil has infected everything about us and the world we live in). It teaches us not to trust ourselves and our desires. So much of the Bible underlines this basic lesson again and again.

So where on earth can we go for the help we all need? Are we irredeemably lost in the fog of human failure? Is there anyone with the 'clear standpoint of experiential purity from which to figure the topic of sexuality out'?[5] This is when the Bible brings us real hope, for in its pages we finally get the help we all need from the only One who perfectly fits that description: Jesus, the Word made flesh.

For part of the good news of Christianity is that the God who created us, who gave us sexuality, has not left us to fend for ourselves when it comes to expressing ourselves sexually in right and confident ways. Instead, he has given us all the help we need in his written word to us and, most of all, in the humanity of his Son. God is not as afraid of talking about sexuality as we are – the Bible is full of sexual imagery and language – and in the person of Jesus he has experienced for himself what it's like to have a sexuality. We haven't been left alone to sort out the mess of our sexualities – in him (and him alone) we have all the help we need.

2

What is sexuality for?

'Did you ask the right questions?' Friends have challenged me when buying some of the more expensive and important things in life, from a mobile phone contract to a car to a home. My problem is that I haven't got a clue what the right questions are in those circumstances, so each time I've had to phone a friend to help me out. Only then did I get the questions – and answers – I needed.

When we Christians (and other interested parties) have opened up the Bible to find out more about sexuality, we've not been asking the right questions. We've been preoccupied with questions such as, 'Who can I have sex with?' and 'When can I have sex with them?' and thought that was all we needed to know. Most of the Christian teaching I received as a teenager revolved around asking and answering these questions (or variations on them) and nothing else really (apart from what actually qualifies as sex). We were taught that we could have sex with someone of the opposite sex (who wasn't a close relation), but only after we had made a public and lifelong commitment to them in a marriage cere-mony. These were clearly and confidently articulated rules, but the reasons for the rules were rarely explained, and as a result they were often ignored. When the question 'Why?' was asked, we were simply told, 'Because God says so!' in a

9

dismissive way that often failed utterly to persuade any of us of the essential good of his commands.

The right question

But *the* question that I think we should all be asking and answering instead is a more profound one: 'What is sexuality *for*?' Answering this question will both help us to make sense of what the Bible teaches *and* what our bodies feel. It will also give us something more positive than a set of rules, as we understand *why* God reserves sex for the lifelong union of a woman and a man, and how that can be good news for both those who are married and for those who, like me, are very much not.

Just think for a moment how, in life, finding out what something is actually *for* is so often the game-changing moment in appreciating and using it properly. Imagine someone handing you a distinctively shaped cylindrical, trowel-like implement that has, confusingly, no ability to carry any soil. It doesn't look like much use to you, so you ask, 'What's it for?' And back comes the answer, 'Planting daffodil and tulip bulbs.' Suddenly it has value; it has a purpose; and you can now make good use of it, knowing what it's there for.

So how would you answer the question, 'What is sexuality for?' I guess most people who've been Christians for a while will confidently trot off three easy answers that are all good and true.

Marital union

Although we may never have succeeded in reading the Bible in a year, we have got as far as Genesis 2 on a number of occasions and so have gate-crashed the first ever wedding. Human sexuality is clearly in play right here at the beginning of human history, before anything at all had gone wrong:

> Then the LORD God made a woman from the rib he had taken out of the man, and he brought her to the man.
> The man said,
>
> 'This is now bone of my bones
>   and flesh of my flesh;
> she shall be called "woman",
>   for she was taken out of man.'
>
> That is why a man leaves his father and mother and is united to his wife, and they become one flesh.
> Adam and his wife were both naked, and they felt no shame.
> (Genesis 2:22–25)

In the very beginning the first man (Adam) meets the first woman (Eve). The immediate result is the first love poem (v. 23) ever written, which doesn't compare well to a Shakespearean sonnet, but it does express Adam's instinctive delight in what he sees, and leads very quickly on to the very first marriage and sexual union (v. 24). In the beginning, boy meets girl. They fall in love at first sight, get married straight away and experience the joy of sex – it's like *Romeo and Juliet*, but with a slightly happier ending.

And this would seem to be human sexuality working as it was made to work by God himself – to draw two people of opposite sex into the lifelong union that is marriage. The Bible makes it clear that, right from the perfect beginning of life on this planet, sexuality is there for marital union. But *why* does this marital union need Adam and Eve to be sexually different? Well, in the beginning, when everything was perfect, marital union was also about . . .

Having children

This is made clear when we turn back a page in the Bible to the creation of humankind and these famous words:

> So God created mankind in his own image,
>   in the image of God he created them;
>   male and female he created them.
>
> God blessed them and said to them, 'Be fruitful and increase in number; fill the earth and subdue it. Rule over the fish in the sea and the birds in the sky and over every living creature that moves on the ground.' (Genesis 1:27–28)

Why does humanity come in two versions: male and female? Why do we have sexual differences between men and women in God's good creation? We share the same human dignity, so why not share exactly the same human bodies? Well, back to those embarrassing biology lessons at school: men and woman have different bodies, and different reproductive organs, so that they can make babies together.

So that, from a biblical point of view, means humanity can fulfil the command given in verse 28 to have children and together to rule this world responsibly on God's behalf.

We know that in this now fallen world not everyone is able to have children – and none of us has cared for the world around us as much as we ought to have done. But 'having children' is still a correct and good answer to the question 'What is sexuality for?' As is . . .

Sharing pleasure

This would, no doubt, be the most popular answer to the question in our society today. But there have been times in the church's long history when the idea of human beings' sexuality bringing them pleasure, even within marriage, has been deeply frowned upon. However, the Bible itself has never been embarrassed about the joy of marital sex. At its heart is a collection of erotic love poetry – the Song of Songs, which (at one level) is an unabashed celebration of the sexual experiences and feelings of a man and a woman. To give just one example, read these verses from one chapter:

I belong to my beloved,
    and his desire is for me.
Come, my beloved, let us go to the countryside,
    let us spend the night in the villages.
Let us go early to the vineyards
    to see if the vines have budded,
if their blossoms have opened,
    and if the pomegranates are in bloom –
    there I will give you my love.

The mandrakes send out their fragrance,
    and at our door is every delicacy,
both new and old,
    that I have stored up for you, my beloved.
(Song of Songs 7:10–13)

This couple are not planning a night-time hike around a nearby National Trust property to see the stars. They are heading into the countryside for sex – pomegranates and mandrakes being aphrodisiacs that they are planning to benefit from. They are looking forward to giving sexual pleasure to each other in ways that God created their bodies to enjoy. God is not a prude when it comes to sex and sexuality – he made them both, and he wants them to be rightly enjoyed and celebrated.

Unsatisfying answers

Now all of the above answers will no doubt sound like good news if you are married to someone of the opposite sex, are able to have children and are enjoying your sex life with your husband or wife. God has given you sexuality for marital union, having children and sharing pleasure, and you are doing all three. Pat yourself on the back (or get your husband or wife to do it for you).

But what if you are married and can't have children or aren't enjoying sex? What if you are single and long to express your sexuality, but have all three expressions closed to you because you are not yet married? What if you were married but are now widowed or divorced, yet still have a living and breathing sexuality? What if you are never going to get married because you are sexually attracted to your own sex and believe that, as a Christian, same-sex sexual relationships are not open to you? These answers are not such good news for you – more of a slap across the face than a pat on the back.

One of the most memorable conversations of my life was with a student I was mentoring over a decade or so ago. He said something like this to me about his struggle to embrace his sexuality towards the end of his teens: 'Why can't God just zap people with a sexuality on their wedding day when he finally allows them to use it? Why give them sexual feelings they have to repress and feel guilty about until the day they get married and are finally allowed to experience what our sexuality is there for?'

Can you imagine the silence that followed this outburst, spoken with quite a lot of feeling? I was stumped by his powerful questions. If sexuality is just for marital union, having children and sharing pleasure with our husband or wife, why are we burdened with sexuality until we are allowed to express it properly? He'd made what felt like a very good point. And what about those of us with a sexuality that we'll *never* get to express in marital union, having children or sharing pleasure with someone of the opposite sex? He thought that things were bad enough for someone like him. What about someone like me?

Just having these much repeated answers to the question 'What is sexuality for?' is so unsatisfying for so many people. It's why so many of them have walked away from the Bible's teaching, from historic Christian sexual ethics. It may be why you are wobbling in your beliefs and behaviour or feeling unable to embrace Christianity for the very first time. To be given such powerful feelings and then to be told that you can never enjoy or express them in any way seems to be both cruel and unliveable.

It *is* cruel and undoable. To answer the key question 'What is sexuality for?' with just these answers – however good and true they are – is to set everyone up for a fall, because these answers are not the whole truth. They are not good enough in and of themselves. God has so much more to say on the subject.

3

What is sexuality really for?

Have you ever read something – a book, an article, a letter, a poem, a text or a paragraph – that's changed your life? Here are just two sentences that have transformed mine:

> the *ultimate* reason (not the only one) why we are sexual is to make God more deeply knowable. The language and imagery of sexuality are the most graphic and most powerful that the Bible uses to describe the relationship between God and his people – both positively (when we are faithful) and negatively (when we are not).[1]

I first read this just a few weeks after that conversation with the student I was mentoring and it blew my mind – and heart – away. Like him, I had basically seen sexuality, my sexual experiences and feelings, as nothing but a curse. I found it difficult to think of any positive reasons for them. With no prospect of a wedding day, I didn't want God just to zap me with a sexuality then – I wanted him to zap my sexuality and take it away for ever. But then these words from the American pastor John Piper helped me to appreciate how sexuality has a good purpose in my life, even if I never enjoy a sexual relationship with anyone.

But what exactly is he saying? Piper is arguing that the chief reason we have a God-given sexuality is to help us grasp the full passion of God's love for us, his people, and the horrific pain he feels when we walk away from him. Our sexual feelings are a reference point for us in communicating the full power of God's loving feelings towards us, and how awful it is when are unfaithful to him.[2]

Appreciating God

Where does Piper get this idea from? It is new to many of us and often when I share it, I get rather concerned looks in response to this strange teaching. But please just read these verses from Ezekiel 16 to see the Bible doing exactly what Piper is describing:

> The word of the LORD came to me: 'Son of man, confront Jerusalem with her detestable practices and say, "This is what the Sovereign LORD says to Jerusalem: your ancestry and birth were in the land of the Canaanites; your father was an Amorite and your mother a Hittite. On the day you were born your cord was not cut, nor were you washed with water to make you clean, nor were you rubbed with salt or wrapped in cloths. No one looked on you with pity or had compassion enough to do any of these things for you. Rather, you were thrown out into the open field, for on the day you were born you were despised.
>
> '"Then I passed by and saw you kicking about in your blood, and as you lay there in your blood I said to you, 'Live!' I made you grow like a plant of the field.

You grew and developed and entered puberty. Your breasts had formed and your hair had grown, yet you were stark naked.

'"Later I passed by, and when I looked at you and saw that you were old enough for love, I spread the corner of my garment over you and covered your naked body. I gave you my solemn oath and entered into a covenant with you, declares the Sovereign LORD, and you became mine.

'"I bathed you with water and washed the blood from you and put ointments on you. I clothed you with an embroidered dress and put sandals of fine leather on you. I dressed you in fine linen and covered you with costly garments. I adorned you with jewellery: I put bracelets on your arms and a necklace round your neck, and I put a ring on your nose, earrings on your ears and a beautiful crown on your head. So you were adorned with gold and silver; your clothes were of fine linen and costly fabric and embroidered cloth. Your food was honey, olive oil and the finest flour. You became very beautiful and rose to be a queen. And your fame spread among the nations on account of your beauty, because the splendour I had given you made your beauty perfect, declares the Sovereign LORD.

'"But you trusted in your beauty and used your fame to become a prostitute. You lavished your favours on anyone who passed by and your beauty became his. You took some of your garments to make gaudy high places, where you carried on your prostitution. You went to him, and he possessed your beauty. You also

took the fine jewellery I gave you, the jewellery made of my gold and silver, and you made for yourself male idols and engaged in prostitution with them. And you took your embroidered clothes to put on them, and you offered my oil and incense before them. Also the food I provided for you – the flour, olive oil and honey I gave you to eat – you offered as fragrant incense before them. That is what happened, declares the Sovereign LORD."'
(Ezekiel 16:1–19)

What story is God telling us in these graphic verses? It's a love story, in which he takes pity on his people in their unloveliness, marries them when they are ready, provides them with everything they need but is then cruelly cuckolded as they run off after idols, sharing his gifts with them. It is a story that connects with us deeply because our sexuality, our capacity for sexual feelings, can feel both God's passion and his pain. It is a story that appals us as we recognize how the wife's behaviour towards her husband is mirrored in our own treatment of our Creator God time and time again.

I don't think I understood the full offence of my own sin, my own rejection of God, until I saw it in these sexual terms – as spiritual adultery towards the God who has given me everything I enjoy, even the things and people I then idolize as substitutes for him. I don't think I had grasped the full wonder of his persistent, gracious love for me until I saw him as a jilted husband who, incredibly, loved me before I ever loved him, and who keeps on loving me even when I have stopped loving him.

It turns out that the thing God has most used to help me appreciate his love for me is sexuality – the sexual feelings that, at times, I've wanted him to take away! If I were not a sexual being, if I didn't feel sexual passion and pain, I wouldn't be able to feel the full intensity of his passionate and painful love for me. So now, when I feel the raw passion of sexual feelings, I take the chance to reflect on the small insight they are giving me into the raw passion of God's love for his people (including me). When I feel the real pain of sexual unfaithfulness, I'm reminded of what we, what I, have done to God himself again and again and again.

Do you see why John Piper can argue that our sexuality exists, most of all, to help us appreciate God's faithful love for us, his unfaithful people – for this powerful spiritual benefit more than anything else? Do you need a bit more convincing? If so, look at another Old Testament prophet, Hosea, and see God using sexual imagery again to communicate his passion and pain. Then, of course, there's a whole book in the Bible in which God's love for us is communicated in unashamedly erotic terms, using sexual language and imagery on every page – the Song of Songs (which we looked at earlier). It's a book that tells the love story of a man and a woman – and it can be understood in just those terms. But throughout church history it has most of all been read as telling the story of God's love for his chosen people symbolically, connecting with our sexuality so that we feel its full passionate power.

I have a confession to make, which is a rather strange one for a celibate man in his mid-forties: I love a cheesy love song. One of my favourites is Andy Williams's rendition of

'Can't take my eyes off you'. In the light of Ezekiel 16, Hosea, Song of Songs and many other passages in Scripture, it's a song that I sometimes imagine the God of the universe singing to us, his dearly loved people.[3] When I preached on the Song of Songs recently, I even played it after a sermon so my church family might grasp that all the great love ballads, which we might dream of being on the receiving end of, are just pale imitations of the great love song that God has been singing to us since before the beginning of time.

Why do I have such powerfully passionate sexual feelings? To make my life miserable because I can't express them in a marriage to someone of the opposite sex? No! They exist to make my life more joyful, as they help me begin to appreciate God's love for me. Why has God made you as a sexual being? To torture you slowly as you struggle to express your sexuality in the right way? No! You have a sexuality so that he can best communicate to you the full intensity of his love for you, so that you can better appreciate how much he can't take his eyes off you.

Trailing heaven

So what is sexuality *really* for? Appreciating God. But that's not all when it comes to its spiritual, its greatest, significance and value:

> God made us as sexual beings – as men and women with a desire for union – precisely to tell the story of his love for us. In the biblical view, the fulfilment of love between the sexes is a great foreshadowing

of something quite literally 'out of this world' – the infinite bliss and ecstasy that awaits us in heaven.[4]

We have sexuality, sexual experiences and feelings so that we can grasp God's love for us *and* to point us to where this world is heading. And where is that? The Bible tells us: the human story begins with a marriage (the first man to the first woman), and it tells us that human history will end with a wedding too – another union in difference (between God's Son, Jesus, and God's people, the church). This is where everything is heading – to an eternal union, the permanent coming together of heaven and earth, and to what sounds like the best wedding reception ever:

Then I heard what sounded like a great multitude, like the roar of rushing waters and like loud peals of thunder, shouting:

'Hallelujah!
    For our Lord God Almighty reigns.
Let us rejoice and be glad
    and give him glory!
For the wedding of the Lamb has come,
    and his bride has made herself ready.
Fine linen, bright and clean,
    was given her to wear.'

(Fine linen stands for the righteous acts of God's holy people.)

Then the angel said to me, 'Write this: Blessed are those who are invited to the wedding supper of the Lamb!' And he added, 'These are the true words of God.'
(Revelation 19:6–9)

Jesus is, of course, the Lamb, the Bridegroom,[5] and God's people – from all times and all places – are the bride. At present we are just walking down the aisle of history on our way to be married to him. Like all good bridegrooms, he is smiling at us down the aisle, encouraging us to keep going until we are standing right by his side.

Sex and marriage in creation are just a trailer for the new creation. Think for a moment of going to a cinema, hearing the Pearl & Dean music and then watching the trailers. What is the purpose of the trailers? Their aim is to make you want to go and see the films they are promoting. Have you noticed how often sex scenes are included in the trailers to make you want to go and see the film itself? I guess this has been shown to be a successful method.

Well, God has put sex and marriage in creation to trail the new creation – to make us want to go and enjoy the full feature that will be eternity. They are just little foretastes of what the real thing will be like. The most perfect of marriages, and the most pleasurable of sexual unions, are but nothing compared to what will be on offer to all of us then. They are passing trailers that have been designed to grab our hearts and make us want to be at the wedding supper of the Lamb – the greatest wedding party ever – to which we're all invited.

When I'm invited to preach at a wedding, I secretly long to be asked to speak on Revelation 19 (or 21) so that I can make this point.[6] I love telling the assembled congregation that they are taking part in what is a dress rehearsal (to change the analogy for a moment) for the real thing. This news is usually greeted with some consternation. Are the couple not really married? Are people going to have to travel across the country *again*? Are the parents of the bride going to have to splash out still more on another wedding? No, I quickly reassure them all. But whenever we rightly celebrate the wedding of a man and a woman, we are taking part in something that is just a demonstration of how wonderful the final marriage will be, with some wedding ceremonies doing this more successfully than others.

That is why I now enjoy going to weddings as a single man in my mid-forties, with no prospect of ever having one of my own. I used to see them as advertisements for a life that would never be mine and, as a result, found them rather painful. I now see them as trailers for an experience that will be mine one day soon – and in a much better way than any of the hundred excellent weddings I have been to over the last twenty-five years. They are a picture of the truly happily-ever-after ending that is possible for any of us who have had our lives joined to Jesus for ever.

4

How does this help us? Part 1

That all sounds rather lovely, but perhaps it is a little bit like a fairy tale? Nice theology but not that helpful in a practical way in our daily struggles with our damaged sexuality. How is this going to help the gay or lesbian among us as we struggle to make sense of the Bible's ban on same-sex marriage and sex? What use is it going to be when you can't take your eyes off that attractive new colleague? What encouragement is it for those of us (married or unmarried) who aren't enjoying any sex at the moment? How does it help those of us who might be addicted to internet porn? We're going to find out.

Living with sexual difference

To many people, including many Christians, the Bible's ban on same-sex marriage and sex just seems very arbitrary. Why do the two bodies involved need to be different, to be male and female? What is the reasonable justification for saying that two men or two women who love each other can't get married and enjoy sex? Our failure to answer these questions well is why many have changed their minds and embraced same-sex marriage. But, when people are shown that opposite-sex marriage and sex are all about modelling the union in difference between Christ and the church, the Bible's

26

teaching makes a lot more sense. Far from being arbitrary or mean, people begin to see it as both essential and appealing.

One of the best places to go to see the importance of sexual difference from God's point of view is Paul's letter to the Ephesians. One of the reasons why many people like the apostle Paul and his letters is because he writes in a wonderfully clear and logical way that is relatively easy to follow (most of the time). But an exception to this general rule would seem to be the end of chapter 5 of Ephesians, when Paul seems to be talking about the marriage of a man and a woman one moment, and then, in the very next sentence, about the relationship between Christ and the church. You want to stop him and ask him to stick to the topic, not wander off to another subject entirely:

> In this same way, husbands ought to love their wives as their own bodies. He who loves his wife loves himself. After all, no one ever hated their own body, but they feed and care for their body, just as Christ does the church – for we are members of his body. 'For this reason a man will leave his father and mother and be united to his wife, and the two will become one flesh.' This is a profound mystery – but I am talking about Christ and the church. However, each one of you also must love his wife as he loves himself, and the wife must respect her husband.
> (Ephesians 5:28–33)

Do you see what I mean? All the clear talk about marriage between a man and a woman and then, in the middle of it all, a sudden claim that he is really talking about the relationship between Jesus (Christ) and his people (the church). Has Paul got himself into a bit of a muddle? Was he one of those preachers who just couldn't resist a red herring? No, he's just demonstrating how closely linked the relationship between a husband and his wife, and the relationship between Christ and his church, are in biblical theology. So much so that quoting the Bible verse which first introduces the concept of human marriage between a man and a woman (Genesis 2:24) immediately triggers in his mind what it points forwards to: the divine marriage of God's Son to God's people. Thinking about the trailer inevitably starts him teaching about the reality too; pondering the dress rehearsal starts him thinking about the opening night. So, in talking about both human and divine marriage at the same time, Paul hasn't muddled the two – they are inextricably linked in his thinking, and in Christian theology.

All of this big-picture teaching has convinced me (and many others) that sexual difference is non-negotiable when it comes to a Christian understanding of sex and marriage. For, although two different people (in looks, personalities, backgrounds) are united in a same-sex marriage, they are not bodily different, and bodies matter far more in Christian theology than we've often thought, because they represent future realities. The different bodies of a man and a woman in marriage represent the union in difference between the divine Jesus and the human church in that ultimate marriage. Sexual difference in sexual intercourse matters, not for some arbitrary reason, but because it is meant to help tell the story of where this world is heading: it's part of the very architecture of the gospel. C. S. Lewis, typically, put it very well for us:

> the kind of equality which implies that the equals are interchangeable (like counters or identical machines) is, among humans, a legal fiction. It may be a useful fiction, but in church we turn our back on fictions. One of the ends for which sex was created was to symbolise to us the hidden things of God. One of the functions of human marriage is to express the nature of the union between Christ and the Church. We have no authority to take the living and seminal figures which God has painted on the canvas of our nature and shift them about as if they were mere geometrical figures.[1]

At one level it would be very lovely for me to meet the man of my dreams, get married to him and enjoy being united with him (including sexually). As a result, I find the attempts to justify this within a biblical framework very appealing.[2] But, increasingly, I think this is a false dream because I would be expressing myself sexually in a way that God has not intended, and so damaging all those involved. This is what sin (living in opposition to God's intentions) always does – it harms people. Same-sex sexual relationships are no exception to this rule. I would be rashly changing the symbols that God himself has given us, in an inevitably unsuccessful bid to please myself: I need to be sexually different from my sexual partner to do what sex is meant to do for me and others. Saying that I am 'married' to someone who is the same sex as me would be a fiction from God's point of view, because I would be personally rearranging how he has decided to place things. And his arrangements are ultimately for my benefit, not least because they point me (and everyone else) forwards, in a beautiful way, to the union in difference that we are all going to enjoy one day, as we who are God's people are married to God's Son for ever.

Knowing that God's insistence on sexual union in difference is not some silly rule that excludes me but, rather, is part and parcel of the gospel story which *includes* me and is for my lasting benefit, helps me to live with my sexuality in a way that I can't begin to tell you.

I've recently been helped further by an increasing number of non-Christian gay voices that are openly expressing the problems caused by a lack of sexual difference in same-sex sexual relationships. Listen to the gay novelist Edmund White reflecting on his sexual experiences:

> It seems to me that two men can never achieve the degree of tongue-and-groove intimacy of a man and a woman. Two men can be best friends, but that's a comfortable arrangement compared to a biological fit – or is it just the reciprocal role-playing? – of a man and a woman.[3]

The gay psychologist Walt Odets talks about the problems that many male same-sex couples whom he's counselled encounter in their sex lives because they are too focused on what he calls 'sport sex' ('focused on novelty, orgasm and demonstrations of prowess and performance'[4]) and don't know how to transition to more healthy 'relationship sex' ('that remains erotically engaging, but also communicates intimacy, affection, and attachment'[5]). He writes:

> straight couples often have an advantage: they have some measure of feminine sensibility in the game, a sensibility much more attuned to emotional expression.
>
> Among gay men I have worked with in therapy, those with no previous sexual experience with women almost invariably have more difficulty in understanding the idea of relationship sex.[6]

Perhaps Daniel Mendelsohn, a gay journalist, puts the case for the importance of sexual difference in a sexual relationship best:

> Sex between men dissolves otherness into sameness . . . there is nothing the partner doesn't know about the other. If the emotional aim of intercourse is a total *knowing* of the other, gay sex may be, in its way, perfect, because in it a total knowledge of the other's experience is, finally, possible. But since the object of that knowledge is already wholly known to each of the parties, the act is also, in a way, redundant. Perhaps it is for this reason that so many of us keep seeking repetition, as if depth were impossible.[7]

The same-sex sexual relationship of my dreams seems less attractive, less possible, as I read of the sexual experiences of these men. The problem is not just that I am 'not allowed' to enjoy marital and sexual union with another man but also this would not properly satisfy me.[8]

From a female perspective, this is backed up by the writer Melinda Selmys, who has been in sexual relationships with both sexes:

It is because of, and not in spite of, the tensions between the sexes that marriage works. Masculinity and femininity each have their vices and strengths. The difficulty when you have two women or two men together is that they understand each other too well, and are thus inclined more to excuse than forgive. That frank bafflement which inevitably sets in, in any heterosexual relationship ('Why on earth would she do that? I just don't understand . . .') never set in throughout all of the years that my girlfriend and I were together – naturally enough. We were both women, and we chose each other because we seemed to be particularly compatible women.[9]

It turns out that sexual difference is important both theologically and experientially if sex is to be properly understood and enjoyed. This must be why our good God has helpfully made sexual difference a non-negotiable in the sexual relationships he permits. His answers to the question 'What is sexuality for?' really help us to live with sexual difference.

Living with human beauty

What has also been of great help to me has been slowly coming to the realization that our attractions to other people are, like everything else about us, a messy mix of both good and bad. I've found that too many Christians only ever feel guilt about their instinctive attraction to human beauty – how they are naturally drawn to beauty in another person or personality. Church teaching has too often made people feel totally ashamed of this instinctive response, rather than helping them to make better sense of it in the light of one famous Bible verse that we have already looked at:

> So God created mankind in his own image,
>   in the image of God he created them;
>   male and female he created them.
> (Genesis 1:27)

When we, as human beings, find ourselves drawn to beauty in other people or their personality, what are we ultimately being drawn to? The image of God in them. Their beauty, in whatever form, is just a mirror of his beauty: the smile on their face has been inherited from him; their kindness to others is just his family likeness. We are being reminded of him, drawn to his beauty, when we recognize beauty in other human beings – and that is a good thing.

Someone who made this point was the Catholic priest Henri Nouwen. In reply to a letter in which a young gay man had described what he was looking for in another man, Nouwen wrote: 'Thank you so much for the expression of your desire and hope. You know already that the young, attractive, affectionate, caring, intelligent, spiritual and socially conscious gay man has only one name: God!'[10] It is a point provocatively made. But the different sorts of beauty that all of us desire and hope for in another human being come from God himself, and so the person we really want and need is God. We should be following what we are drawn to back to its source, and benefit from the real, lasting version and not the pale, passing imitation that all human beings are. As someone else has put it, 'All beauty is a breadcrumb path that leads us to Christ.'[11]

For years I used to be paralysed with guilt when I even noticed an obviously beautiful man. I can remember watching a TV drama with my parents, who commented separately on the incredible good looks of the young lead actor. I had already noticed – and felt ashamed at having done so. But that both my parents had noticed and commented on it reminded me that he was objectively beautiful to the heterosexual man and woman sitting with me, so for me to feel bad about noticing that was just foolish. If I'd begun to idolize him, worship him and want to consume him sexually, I would have been sinning and have had something to repent of. But my instinctive attraction to his beauty was natural and nothing to be ashamed of. It actually has very little to do with my particular experience of sexuality and more to do with the fact that God has wired us all to appreciate the beauty he has scattered all over creation – in sunsets, trees, art, music, actions and words – and in other people. He has designed beauty to stop us in our tracks and bring us back to him.

We need to appreciate, increasingly, that any time we're instinctively attracted to another human being is a call to worship – a call to worship the Creator of the beauty, not the bearer of it. I'm slowly training myself to do that when I come across beauty in any form, but most especially human beauty. I want to honestly recognize that my track record is one of idolatry, of worshipping another creature rather than the Creator. But the experience can do me good if I end up worshipping, instead, the God whose greater beauty I have just caught a brief glimpse of.

I recently came across a prayer that puts all of this thinking in a wonderfully usable form.

Upon seeing a beautiful person
Lord, I praise you for divine beauty
reflected in the form of this person.
Now train my heart so that my response
to their beauty would not be twisted
downward into envy or desire,
but would instead be directed upward
in worship of you, their Creator –
as was your intention for all such beauty
before the breaking of the world.[12]

Amen! We all need to be learning and using this prayer to see how that instinctive moment of attraction to a creature can become a moment of instinctive praise of our Creator.

5

How does this help us? Part 2

Are you now beginning to see how Christian theology on sex and sexuality is incredibly helpful in the midst of our real-life experiences and questions? Even in a short book we need two separate chapters on how it can help us – which I hope makes an important point. It saddens me that so many Christians haven't ever been connected to the help they most need in living with their sexual experiences and feelings, help that comes, of course, from the person who knows them best – God himself.

Living with sexual pleasure

Our society – through images and voices – is constantly advertising the joy of sex. Many people think that sexuality is only about sexual pleasure. The quest for it is no longer a taboo subject, but has become the preoccupation of numerous articles, conversations and lives. For many people it is what human flourishing is all about. So the lack of sexual pleasure in the life of the single Christian is probably one of the most off-putting ideas for the non-Christian investigating the claims and promises of Jesus.

This lack of sexual pleasure is also one of the most off-putting realities of the faithful life for single Christians themselves. I can recall a conversation with a student I was mentoring that especially brought this home to me. We were talking about the promised return of Jesus, an event that we Christians are taught to long for[1] because it will be then, and then only, when he will finally make 'everything sad . . . come untrue'.[2] But my young friend confessed that he wanted Jesus to return only *after* he married, because he didn't want to miss out on the joy of sex.

I recall mocking him a bit in my not too pastoral response. Was he really fearing that he would be kicking himself for all of a blissful eternity because he'd not enjoyed a few moments of ecstasy in the here and now? If he somehow knew that Jesus was returning the next day, would he immediately get married and have sex before it was too late for that sort of pleasure? 'Yes' was his honest reply. It turned out he had never grasped the reality that temporary sexual pleasure in the here and now is just a foretaste of the everlasting pleasures which will be ours in the world to come. But this was because he'd never been taught this by me, the pastor who was mocking his raw response to my questions.

We're back to the idea of sex and marriage being a trailer for the new creation. But we are now seeing how this reality can help those of us who are not experiencing, and perhaps never will experience, the joy of sex in the present. It turns out that, if sex is just a foretaste of the real thing, it doesn't matter so much if we miss out on it now. No-one who gets to enjoy a really good film in its entirety kicks themselves for having missed seeing the enticing short trailer. None of us will be regretting what we haven't yet experienced here and now when we get to enjoy the full reality of what it's been pointing forwards to: the marriage, the union in difference, between Christ and his church. It is a union that will involve more pleasure, happiness, intimacy and ecstasy than any sexual relationship beforehand.

Knowing that sex is there to trail heaven is also good news for those who aren't enjoying sex – and, the surveys inform us, there are a lot of us. I find that this news goes down well not only with single Christians but also with Christians who are married but have found sex hasn't lived up to the hype or simply isn't happening any more. It's also been good news for those who are no longer married as a result of death or divorce. Contrary to the world's narrative, we are not missing out on the real thing that makes life worth living, just an imitation designed to point us to where the real thing is to be found.

Of course, this is also good news for those who are enjoying sex within marriage at the moment. To put it explicitly, the best orgasm you have ever had is just a foretaste of the sort of pleasure the future holds. If that's just a shadow, think how much better the reality will one day be.

But that reality will then be experienced by *all* who are united to Christ – the married and single, the widowed and divorced, the gay and straight. This means that all of us can start putting sex in its right place here and now, and stop our idolatry of sex destroying ourselves and others. I recently came across these words in a book intriguingly entitled *Why Sex Doesn't Matter* by the secular author Olivia Fane:

When I told a friend that I was going to write this book – a close friend who has known me for twenty years – she said to me, 'Olivia, I have never seen you so angry. Where has your anger come from?' I told her that I had been abused, not by another without my permission, neither by Jimmy Saville, nor a film producer, nor a priest. Rather, I have been abused by the dominant ideology of the day: *that sex is important and profound and you are obliged to join in.*[3]

We have all been on the receiving end of that abusive ideology, haven't we? It's led to young people harming themselves by losing their virginity too early,[4] self-harming because they haven't yet lost their virginity, others thinking that life without sex isn't worth living any more or destroying other people's lives so they can enjoy sex right now. In the rest of the book, Fane is painfully honest about the damage this thinking has done in her own life, and anyone like me who is involved in pastoral ministry knows that she is part of a majority, not a minority, in our society today.

Part of the good news of the Christian story is that sex is important and profound, *but you are not obliged to join in.* You don't ever have to have sex because the reason why it is so important and profound is what it points us forwards to, not what it is in and of itself. Sexual pleasure is just a foretaste, and the lack, or experience, of it should make us look forward to a great day:

Then I saw 'a new heaven and a new earth', for the first heaven and the first earth had passed away, and there was no longer any sea. I saw the Holy City, the new Jerusalem, coming down out of heaven from God,

prepared as a bride beautifully dressed for her husband.
And I heard a loud voice from the throne saying, 'Look!
God's dwelling-place is now among the people, and he
will dwell with them. They will be his people, and God
himself will be with them and be their God. "He will
wipe every tear from their eyes. There will be no more
death" or mourning or crying or pain, for the old order
of things has passed away.'
(Revelation 21:1–4)

On that day no-one will be mourning their lack of sex
on the first earth or the end of sex in the new one.[5] Instead,
we will all be enjoying the lasting blissful union to which
sex has pointed us. This time it will be a perfect and permanent union with no death or mourning, crying or pain.
We'll all be enjoying the reality, with none of the sad, all
too common negative effects of the previous imitation.
I can't wait!

But, to bring us down to earth with a bump, that day may
not happen soon. And, in the meantime, how does all of this
help us to live with sexual temptation?

Living with sexual temptation

How does knowing what sexuality is really for help us with
what often feels like the toughest of battles – saying no to the
sex we often want right now? How does it help us live with
sexual feelings that so often bring death, mourning, crying
and pain into our daily lives in the here and now?

If sex is so important and profound in the Christian story,
if it's designed to communicate both God's passionate and

faithful love for us and our eternal destiny to be united to him in Christ, we should hardly be surprised that it has become such a battleground. If sexual faithfulness within marriage is meant to help us grasp God's faithfulness to us, of course the evil one wants as much sexual unfaithfulness within marriage as possible. If the marriage and sex lives of a man and a woman are meant to be a trailer for the union in difference between Christ and the church, of course God's enemy wants us to feel free to change things without realizing the eternal consequences. When you grasp how much sexuality and sex matter to the gospel, it should stop being such a surprise that the church is so often in a mess when it comes to these areas of belief and behaviour. The theologian Beth Felker Jones helps us to understand this:

> The way Christians do – and don't – have sex is anchored in the deepest truth about reality, and it witnesses to the reality of a God who loves and is faithful to his people. More than that, Christian sexual ethics reflect reality because they make sense of the kind of creatures God made us to be, and so those sexual ethics offer us a way to really flourish as human beings.[6]

So this is where you'd attack if you wanted to destroy – as much as possible, as quickly as possible – an individual Christian, or a whole church, or a denomination, or the entire human race. Sadly, we know this from our own lives, from churches we're part of and from the lives of the communities around us. The devil knows this most of all and has been using this information down through the generations to inflict huge damage in this area of human existence more than any other. He's found our weakest spot and he's kept on pummelling it.

This explains why Paul uses the language he does in writing to the Corinthian church about sexual immorality (any sexual activity outside heterosexual marriage). It's not that he's got a thing against sex – he encourages married couples to keep having sex in 1 Corinthians 7. It's that he grasps just how damaging it can be. That's why he uses strong language like this in the previous chapter:

> Flee from sexual immorality. All other sins a person commits are outside the body, but whoever sins sexually, sins against their own body. Do you not know that your bodies are temples of the Holy Spirit, who is in you, whom you have received from God? You are not your own; you were bought at a price. Therefore honour God with your bodies.
>
> (1 Corinthians 6:18–20)

Sex itself is not something to be afraid of, but the damage that the wrong use of it does to us means that we should run away from sexual sin. We should never forget the spiritual power of our bodies and what we do (or don't do) with them matters because God himself, having paid the greatest price for us, now lives in them. In chapter 7 Paul goes on to talk about a married couple's bodies belonging to each other. Here he reminds us all that our bodies belong primarily to God himself.

And the devil hates that because they used to belong to him. So, when you and I feel that our bodies are battlefields, we are experiencing a spiritual reality. God has taken up residence in us, through his Spirit, but the devil is laying siege to us to try to win us back. That sexual temptation is the greatest battle in our lives is a sign not that we're not really Christians (as we sometimes fear), but that we are, and that, as a result, the evil one is throwing his deadliest weapons at us.

It used to baffle me that the times when I was speaking or writing on sexuality were the times of greatest temptation for me personally. Writing a chapter like this feels like a spiritual boxing match from which I emerge bloodied. But of course I do. In writing this, in reading this, in trying to live out all of this, we are fighting for our spiritual lives and the future life of the gospel in our communities. Don't be surprised if it's the toughest battle you will face, but be encouraged.

6

What does God do to help us?

Are you beginning to see and feel just how much knowing what God says our sexuality is for can *really* help us? And help *all* of us, whatever our experience of sexuality has been, however we might seek to define ourselves?

God has given us all the gift of sexuality so that we might experience important and profound things that we'd never understand without it. As a result, on a good day, when his vision for it is shining clearest in my heart and mind, I am grateful for God's gift of purposeful sexuality.

But I've got to confess that, on a bad day – when I'm weary in the battle against sexual temptation, when I feel alone, with nothing but my unfulfilled sexual fantasies to keep me company – I'm not grateful to God. Instead, I feel quite resentful towards him. What does God know about how hard it is to try and express sexual feelings rightly? What does he know about the power of sexual desire? When has he ever been tired and alone and had to say 'No!' to a possible sexual encounter that has just presented itself? What does God do to help us? He hasn't really got a clue about what he's asking of me, or of you – has he?

Jesus is on the inside

Except, of course, that, in his Son, Jesus, God himself became a man. As Jesus' best friend John famously put it:

> The Word became flesh and made his dwelling among us. We have seen his glory, the glory of the one and only Son, who came from the Father, full of grace and truth. (John 1:14)

God became a human being, which means that God became a sexual being (the two go together). John stresses this in his choice of words.[1] The Jesus that John shared his life with for three years was a real man, and so his humanity would have included sexual feelings, in other words, a sexuality. And in writing his Gospel, John seems to want to make it very clear that this was part of Jesus and his humanity. He wants his readers to get that Jesus knows what it is like to be a sexual being. He lived in a sexual world in which he would have experienced sexual desire and yet never damaged himself, or anyone else, with his use of his sexuality. Part of the beauty of Jesus is that he knows what it's like to be like you and me – in our humanity, living with sexuality – and yet he didn't muck it up in the way we do. As the writer to the Hebrews famously explains:

> For we do not have a high priest who is unable to feel sympathy for our weaknesses, but we have one who has been tempted in every way, just as we are – yet he did not sin.
> (Hebrews 4:15)

One of the ancient creeds helpfully puts it like this: Jesus was 'in all things like unto us, without sin'.[2] God in Christ is, incredibly, on the inside when it comes to human sexuality, yet he never damaged anyone in his expression of it.

But where does John clearly communicate all of this? Have you missed the section about Jesus' sexuality in the early pages of John's Gospel? Well, I did for years, until I reread John chapter 4 with the help of New Testament scholar Andy Angel,[3] and saw how Jesus' meeting with the Samaritan woman at the well is, in part, set up as a romantic meeting with sexual expectations. Angel concludes his book on Jesus' sexuality with these words:

> John deliberately brings out Jesus' experience of sexual desire in the frailty that is common to all of us. Those of us for whom questions about faith, sex and sexuality arise from our experience can heave a sigh of relief: the God whose commands we struggle with, and to whom we pray in and about our difficulties, understands sexual desire from experience. He is not only 'gentle and humble in heart' as he disciples us, but he has more than a rough idea of what we are going through.[4]

Jesus is on the inside when it comes to sexuality – because he has one. During his time on this earth, he lived with his sexuality in a finite body like yours and mine, yet he always thought, desired and acted perfectly.

John highlights Jesus' humanity as he begins his account of his conversation with a Samaritan woman:

> Jacob's well was there, and Jesus, tired as he was from
> the journey, sat down by the well. It was about noon.
> (John 4:6)

John wants us to register that Jesus is physically exhausted,
that, like you and me, there were times when he could go no
further, when he was spent. And this is the context into
which a woman walks:

> When a Samaritan woman came to draw water, Jesus
> said to her, 'Will you give me a drink?' (His disciples
> had gone into the town to buy food.)
> (vv. 7–8)

Jesus' humanity is stressed yet again – he needs a drink, like
any other tired human being resting in the noonday sun. But
John also wants us to note that Jesus and this woman are all
alone – he carefully points out that the disciples (himself
included) were all off on a shopping trip.

Why make sure that his readers grasp that Jesus is tired
and alone? Well, when do human beings most often muck
up sexually? When they are tired and/or alone. There are
many ancient stories that demonstrate this, and countless
contemporary accounts too. That is why so much adultery
happens on business trips, and why pornography is accessed
most often when people are feeling exhausted and isolated.
We tend to fail sexually when we no longer have the energy
to resist, when we can kid ourselves that nobody else will ever
know. Nearly all the times that I have mucked up sexually
have been when I was in Jesus' situation in John chapter 4 –
when I was tired and alone. And, from numerous pastoral

conversations I've had, that would seem to be almost universally true.

OK, so Jesus is a human being, as in 'the Word became flesh' – a sexual being. He is tired and alone. A woman appears. Surely it's a bit far-fetched to see this as the beginning of a potentially sexually charged encounter? Especially one involving Jesus, who is perfect. The very idea might shock you. Isn't this a classic case of a twenty-first-century obsession with sex reading something back into an innocent first-century text?

Except that it's actually the wider context of the beginning of John's Gospel that introduces this expectation, and some sexual tension. I, for one, didn't read anything sexual into John 4 until this context was pointed out to me. Just ponder who Jesus is being portrayed as at this stage of John's Gospel. What is the first miracle that John (in contrast to the other Gospel writers) records? It is Jesus doing the bridegroom's job for him by providing the wine at a wedding feast at Cana (2:1–11). How does John the Baptist describe him in chapter 3? As 'the bridegroom' (3:29). Jesus is being presented as a man looking for a wife.

Then there's a wider biblical context that we should be aware of too. As Jesus meets a woman at a well in John chapter 4, he finds himself in the biblical equivalent of a singles bar. It was at a well that we first met Isaac's wife-to-be, Rebekah (Genesis 24), where Jacob met his first love, Rachel (Genesis 29) and where Moses met his wife Zipporah (Exodus 2). In the Bible, wells are romantic places, the sort of context in which you might meet the one who will become your wife.

All of this means that if this were a film, the romantic music would be playing by now and we'd all be thinking we know what's about to happen. This is a set-up: the first-century equivalent of the 'meet cute'[5] of contemporary romantic film and fiction: marriage and sex (in one order or the other) are surely just around the corner. The couple in question simply need to discover where the narrative context, the romantic location, is inevitably drawing them.

Confirmation that we are not reading all this back into the text comes from the disciples on their return from the shops. They clearly see Jesus as a sexual being and are immediately worried about what he might have been getting up to with this woman:

> Just then his disciples returned and were surprised to find him talking with a woman. But no one asked, 'What do you want?' or 'Why are you talking with her?' (v. 27)

John records – he was, of course, one of them – that they instinctively (but internally) questioned both Jesus' motives and actions in chatting with the woman at this well. Back then you broke the rule about not talking to the opposite sex alone for one reason only, so what has been going on here? They think they know what's been going on, and they are shocked.

Jesus gets it right

But Jesus and the Samaritan woman smash their (and our) expectations. There has been no marriage proposal, no sex.

Just a conversation in which Jesus broke down contemporary racial, religious and gender barriers (4:9), insightfully offered the woman the spiritual refreshment she had been thirsting for (4:10–14) and declared himself to be the source of all the wisdom we need (4:25–26). She doesn't rush home to show off her engagement ring or to rate Jesus' sexual performance, but to declare: 'Come, see a man who told me everything I've ever done. Could this be the Messiah?' (v. 29).

It turns out that, although Jesus is a man, a sexual being, tired and alone, he behaves differently from other men in those circumstances. He changes the expected narrative and handles his sexuality differently – with total integrity. He does not propose marriage or seek to satisfy himself with the woman sexually, but instead offers her the spiritual satisfaction she's been looking for all her life: 'whoever drinks the water I give them will never thirst. Indeed, the water I give them will become in them a spring of water welling up to eternal life' (v. 14). Jesus is all about what is good for her, not him. Interestingly, he does not treat her as a threat to his sexual purity, but is willing to sit and talk with her in a context where both her race and gender would have made that scandalous. He is willing to be her friend despite the raised eyebrows. He is the 'the one', but not in the way we were expecting.

If you are a woman, the Jesus you meet here is the perfect man who will not treat you as a sexual object to please himself. Instead, he is a man who wants to serve you by giving you spiritual water that will satisfy you eternally. He will not act towards you as if you are a sexual threat to his integrity. Instead, here is a man who is willing to talk with you, answer your questions and gently tell you the truth – be your friend.

If you are a man, the Jesus you meet here is a man like you who provides you with a perfect example to follow in his treatment of women. Being tired and alone is not an excuse to take advantage of women in reality or online. Instead, you too are being pointed to the lasting satisfaction that Jesus offers you in himself. You are to serve women – they do not exist just to please you sexually. You should not always run away from women as if they were all a threat to your godliness, but instead seek to grow a Christlikeness that is able to act with complete integrity towards them, just as Jesus befriends the woman here.[6]

In John chapter 4 we are deliberately confronted with the man Jesus in a romantically and potentially sexually charged encounter with a woman. But it is one that has been set up to confound our expectations. John's aim is to introduce us all to someone like us, but who, unlike us, has got his sexuality right. We started this book by sharing our need for someone just like Jesus, who has a 'clear standpoint of experiential purity from which to figure the topic of sexuality out'.[7] Jesus Christ is that someone. John 4 encourages us to learn from him, and to point the world around us to him. He – and he alone – provides us with the help we desperately need.

We receive Jesus' sexual history

Of course, the help we all need when it comes to our sexuality starts with forgiveness – forgiveness for the damage we have caused ourselves and others with our sexuality; forgiveness of those who have damaged us with their sexuality; and forgiveness for the damage our misuse of our sexuality has done to our relationship with God. Too many of us feel that our sexuality is too damaged to repair. We desperately wish that our sexual history could be deleted as swiftly as our internet history seems to be, but that doesn't feel possible.

Except that, with Jesus, it is. When we acknowledge our broken record, we are given his perfect record in exchange. At the heart of the good news that he embodies is the promise that we get to trade our sexual history for his. Reread this famous verse specifically with your unwanted sexual history in mind:

> God made him who had no sin to be sin for us, so that
> in him we might become the righteousness of God.
> (2 Corinthians 5:21)

We get to swap sexual histories with Jesus. He gets all our sexual sins: our lust, fantasies, porn addiction, sex outside marriage, selfish sex within marriage, sexual abuse, sexual repression (only you will know precisely what he bears for you). And what do we get in return? We get all Jesus' sexual purity: his self-sacrificial, perfect sexual integrity as he chats with the Samaritan woman, his treatment of her as a real person and not as a sexual threat. We get Jesus' perfect sexual history.

The reformer Martin Luther helps us to feel this as he picks up the biblical imagery of our marital union with Christ to illustrate what happens when we put our faith in Jesus:

Christ is full of grace, life, and salvation, while the soul is full of sins, death, and damnation. Now let faith enter the picture, and sins, death, and damnation are Christ's, while grace, life, and salvation will be the soul's. For if Christ is the bridegroom, he must take upon himself that which are [*sic*] his bride's, and he in turn bestows on her all that is his. If he gives her his body and very self, how shall he not give her all that is his? And if he takes the body of his bride, how shall he not take all that is hers?[8]

All of this, incredibly, means that, for those of us who have put our faith and trust in Jesus Christ: when God looks at you and me, he sees Jesus' sexual purity, not our sexual sin. And that is true of us yesterday, today and for ever because we are now permanently in him. We might feel like sexually damaged goods as we review the past and the present, and we will damage ourselves and others sexually in the future. But, whatever we've done or whatever we might do, we have now been united to Christ: our sexual history is his, and our sexual future is his too.

So, although there will always be things for us to repent of, there is no need for us to feel permanently crushed by sexual guilt and shame, because Jesus has taken our guilt and shame for us. On the cross he felt it, and through the cross he paid for it completely. It is now gone for ever. We are perfect in God's sight. This is the best of news, for, as Adam Smith once wrote, 'Man naturally desires, not only to be loved, but to be lovely.'[9] In Christ, we are now both.

We receive Jesus' constant help

And that is not all. It gets better, for with Jesus

> God didn't simply offer you legal forgiveness. Praise
> him that he did that. But he offered you something
> much more profound. He offered you himself. He knew
> that your need was so great that it wouldn't be enough
> to simply forgive you. He literally needed to unzip
> you and get inside you, or you would never be what you
> were supposed to be and do what you were supposed
> to do.[10]

We need more than divine forgiveness. We need a divine
friend, someone who will be with us constantly as we seek
to inhabit our sexual bodies as Jesus inhabited his sexual
body, someone who knows what it is to be like us, but who,
unlike us, didn't get it wrong, someone who tells us what is
to be done and then sticks around to help. Wonderfully,
with all his previous inside knowledge and experience, Jesus
is now in the business of helping us to express our sexuality
purposefully as he lives inside us. By his Spirit, he now
dwells within us and is working to help us use our bodies,
our sexuality, as he used his: self-sacrificially to point
others to where lasting satisfaction is to be found. We have
not been left alone but have – in Christ alone – all the
resources we need to change. Remember how Paul movingly
put it:

> I have been crucified with Christ and I no longer live,
> but Christ lives in me. The life I now live in the body,

> I live by faith in the Son of God, who loved me and
> gave himself for me.
> (Galatians 2:20)

This verse reminds us beautifully both of God's past forgiveness, through the cross of Christ, and of God's presence
now, through our union with Christ. The danger of reading
(or writing) a book on purposeful sexuality is that we all
end it simply by resolving to change ourselves in response
to what God has said and done for us.[11] Paul here reminds
us that Christian change is achieved by Christ living
through us, making us more like him. As a result, the first
thing we need to do if we're to form a more purposeful
sexuality is to ask for his help. He's on hand to give it (he
lives on the job): my – our – problem is that we so rarely
remember that and act as if we're on our own. So much of
our time and energy are given to self-help methods of
change instead of accessing the divine help that is on tap
inside us.

Hopefully, this book will have given you a short Christian
introduction to what purposeful sexuality looks like, but
remember that only Christ is in a position to help you live it
out. So here's a prayer for the help that you, and indeed all of
us, now need to receive from him:

> Father God, I praise you for the good gift of
>   purposeful sexuality.
> Forgive me for the ways in which I have
>   damaged myself, others, you, in my wrong
>   use of it.

Thank you that you have, most of all, given me
sexual feelings to help me appreciate your love
for me in Christ.

To begin to feel the joy there will be when all your
people are united to him for ever.

May your Son, Jesus, by his Spirit living in me, now
help me to enjoy your good gift of sexuality more
purposefully.

I know I can't do that on my own – thank you that
I don't need to.

Trusting in Jesus' forgiveness and help, I pray in his
name. Amen.

Questions for reflection

By yourself, or in a prayer triplet or a small group, consider the following questions when you come to the end of each chapter.

1 How has this chapter connected with your experiences and feelings?
2 How has this chapter given you hope?
3 How are you going to live this out in the light of that hope?

Notes

Introduction: What are we talking about?

1 William Maxwell, *Over by the River and Other Stories* (Nonpareil Books, 1984), p. 85.

2 Cambridge Dictionary, available online at: <https://dictionary.cambridge.org/dictionary/english/sexuality> (accessed 28 June 2020).

3 This book may be a challenging read for those who are asexual, because it will focus on feelings that you do not have, and because there is not the space within a short book to give any real attention to the questions you might be living with. My apologies, but do get in contact with Living Out (at: <www.livingout.org>).

4 Véronique Mottier, *Sexuality: A very short introduction* (Oxford University Press, 2008), p. 31.

5 Ed Shaw, *The Plausibility Problem: The church and same-sex attraction* (IVP, 2015; published as *Same-Sex Attraction and the Church: The surprising plausibility of the celibate life*, 2015, InterVarsity Press, in the USA).

Chapter 1: Why is talking about sexuality so difficult?

1 To complicate things further, some of these labels are used to describe different sexual feelings, while others are more about different experiences of gender. A helpfully exhaustive glossary of contemporary terms can be found online at: <www.stonewall.org.uk/help-advice/faqs-and-glossary/glossary-terms> (accessed 23 October 2020).

2 As evidenced by the increasing use of the term 'pansexual', 'a person whose romantic and/or sexual attraction towards others is not limited by sex or gender' (see: https://stonewall.org.uk/help-advice/faqs-and-glossary/glossary-terms>, accessed 20 September 2020).

3 Ephraim Radner, *A Time to Keep: Theology, mortality and the shape of a human life* (Baylor University Press, 2016), p. 44.

4 Jessica Martin, *Holiness and Desire* (Canterbury Press, 2020), p. 89.

5 Radner, *A Time to Keep*, p. 44.

Chapter 3: What is sexuality really for?

1 John Piper, 'Sex and the supremacy of Christ: Part one', in John Piper and Justin Taylor (eds), *Sex and the Supremacy of Christ* (Crossway, 2005), p. 26.

2 But what if you are asexual – that is, if you don't have any powerful sexual feelings and so don't experience this personally? I've been asked this question often, and have had a few chances to talk about it with people who describe themselves as asexual. Here's the beginning of an answer: I think asexual people are still able to appreciate the power of sexual feelings, both as they see them affect others and as they (sometimes) feel some sort of lack or gap in themselves.

3 Psalm 32:8 is just one biblical justification for this.

4 Christopher West, *Fill These Hearts: God, sex and the universal longing* (Image, 2012), p. 11.

5 See John 3:28–29 and Matthew 9:15 for some other occasions when this language is used.

6 Please take this hint if you ever ask me to preach at your wedding.

Chapter 4: How does this help us? Part 1

1 C. S. Lewis, 'Priestesses in the Church?', in *Essay Collection: Faith, Christianity and the church* (HarperCollins, 2002), p. 401. *Essay Collection* by C. S. Lewis © copyright CS Lewis Pte Ltd 2000. Used with permission.

2 The most powerful, yet still unconvincing, argument would be Matthew Vines' *God and the Gay Christian: The biblical case in support of same-sex relationships* (Convergent, 2014).

3 Edmund White, *My Lives* (Bloomsbury, 2005), p. 165.

4 Walt Odets, *Out of the Shadows: Reimagining gay men's lives* (Allen Lane, 2019), p. 238.

5 Odets, *Out of the Shadows*, p. 238.

6 Odets, *Out of the Shadows*, p. 239.

7 Daniel Mendelsohn, *The Elusive Embrace: Desire and the riddle of identity* (Vintage, 1999), p. 73.

8 What I'm not saying is that there is no such thing as enjoyable gay sex – these secular gay voices do not question that. But they do raise interesting questions about why gay sex struggles to satisfy its participants in the longer term. This is perhaps why so many permanent and stable gay relationships seem to develop into committed friendships, in which sex is increasingly enjoyed elsewhere or not at all.

9 Melinda Selmys, *Sexual Authenticity: An intimate reflection on homosexuality and Catholicism* (Our Sunday Visitor, 2009), p. 117.

10 Henri J. M. Nouwen, *Love, Henri: Letters on the spiritual life* (Hodder & Stoughton, 2016), p. 343.

11 Steve DeWitt, *Eyes Wide Open: Enjoying God in everything* (Credo, 2012), p. 107.

12 Douglas Kaine McKelvey, *Every Moment Holy* (Rabbit Room Press, 2017), p. 249. Prayer © copyright Douglas Kaine McKelvey. Used with permission of Rabbit Room Press.

Chapter 5: How does this help us? Part 2

1 Revelation 22:20.

2 J. R. R. Tolkien, *The Lord of the Rings* (Unwin, 1968), p. 988.

3 Olivia Fane, *Why Sex Doesn't Matter* (Mensch, 2020), p. 160.

4 The lyrics of Jason Mraz's 'Love for a child' are haunting on this.

5 See Mark 12:25.

6 Beth Felker Jones, *Faithful: A theology of sex* (Zondervan, 2015), p. 17.

Chapter 6: What does God do to help us?

1 'When John describes the physical humanity of Jesus, he does so by using a word that he also uses in the immediate context to refer to sexual desire. Through his choice of words, John suggests that sexual desire was part of God's human experience' (Andy Angel, *Intimate Jesus: The sexuality of God incarnate*, SPCK, 2017, p. 25).

2 Thanks to Andrew Bunt for pointing me to the Creed of Chalcedon (AD 451) (available online at: <https://bible.org/illustration/creed-chalcedon-ad-451>, accessed 4 September 2020).

3 Much of this chapter has been heavily influenced by chapter 3 of Andy's excellent book *Intimate Jesus*. I don't agree with everything he says, but have been massively helped by his refreshing reading of John chapter 4 in the wider context of chapters 1 to 3, and the Old Testament background he draws on.

4 Angel, *Intimate Jesus,* p. 98.

5 Thanks to Dani Treweek for pointing this out. 'The "meet cute" is Hollywood screenwriters' name for a standard plot device in which a couple meet in a way that's charming, ironic, or just generally amusing' (John Carvill, 'Clip joint: The top five "meet cutes"', *The Guardian*, 23 January 2013 (available online at: <www.theguardian.com/film/filmblog/2013/jan/23/clip-joint-meet-cute>, accessed 21 August 2020).

6 I am here consciously contradicting what has become known as the 'Billy Graham rule'. The American evangelist famously avoided being alone with any woman apart from his wife. He had his own good reasons for this, but it has become one of the many extra-biblical rules of evangelicalism. Aimee Byrd's *Why Can't We Be Friends? Avoidance is not purity* (P&R, 2018) is a helpful place to explore the damage this has caused and better approaches.

7 Radner, *A Time to Keep,* p. 44.

8 Martin Luther, *The Freedom of a Christian*, trans. Mark Tranvik (Fortress Press, 2008), p. 62. Thanks to Matthew Mason for pointing me to these words.

9 Quoted in Mark Vernon, *The Meaning of Friendship* (Palgrave Macmillan, 2010), p. 35.

10 Paul David Tripp, *Whiter than Snow: Meditations on sin and mercy* (Crossway, 2008), p. 103.
11 I'm grateful to Grant Macaskill for alerting me to this danger, in his *Living in Union with Christ: Paul's Gospel and Christian moral identity* (Baker, 2019). Thanks again to Matthew Mason for pointing me in this direction.

Acknowledgments

The dedication and footnotes acknowledge many of my debts in writing this short book. Huge thanks are also due to those who kindly gave their feedback on various drafts: Adam, Andrew, Andy, Andy, Caleb, Dani, Eleanor, Fliss, Geoff, Hannah, Hilary, John, Julian, Lily, Matthew, Nat, Ollie and Sue. Responsibility for the final version, of course, rests with me alone. My church family at Emmanuel City Centre in Bristol, and the team at Living Out (<www.livingout.org>), have been very kind in allowing me to test out my ideas on them. This book was written during 2020, so I'm grateful to all my family and friends who have kept me going during these testing lockdown times.

Further reading

The footnotes point you in many different directions. Here are some more focused recommendations.

The two most significant early influences on my theology of sexuality were from very different traditions: John Piper (Protestant) and Christopher West (Roman Catholic). Intriguingly, though, they both say very similar things in the following books:

John Piper and Justin Taylor, ed., *Sex and the Supremacy of Christ* (Crossway, 2005).

Christopher West, *Fill These Hearts: God, sex and the universal longing* (Image, 2012).

Since then I've been especially helped by books from other Christian theologians, which include:

Andy Angel, *Intimate Jesus: The sexuality of God incarnate* (SPCK, 2017).

J. Budziszewski, *On the Meaning of Sex* (ISI Books, 2012).

Beth Felker Jones, *Faithful: A theology of sex* (Zondervan, 2015).

The poetry of John Donne (for example, Holy Sonnet XIV, 'Batter my heart, three-person'd God') and the stories of Wendell Berry (see his novel *Jayber Crow* and short story

'A Desirable Woman') have been influential in applying all of this to my affections.

The failure of the sexual revolution has been tragically highlighted for me by two secular studies:

Mark Regnerus and Jeremy Uecker, *Premarital Sex in America: How young Americans meet, mate and think about marrying* (OUP, 2011).
Matthew Todd, *Straight Jacket: Overcoming society's legacy of gay shame* (Black Swan, 2018).

For anyone seeking to better communicate God's purposeful sexuality to others, I would highly recommend these books from two friends of mine:

Glynn Harrison, *A Better Story: God, sex and human flourishing* (IVP, 2016).
Jason Roach, *Swipe Up: A better way to do love, sex and relationships* (Good Book Company, 2019).

Living Out

We help people, churches
and society talk about
faith and sexuality.

livingout.org

Lightning Source UK Ltd.
Milton Keynes UK
UKHW021528260121
377699UK00010B/2440